FOR EVERY SEASON THERE IS A TIME FOR...

A TABLE OF CONTENTS . . .

A FOREWORD . . .

What an interesting project this has been - the opportunity to set contemporary praise music as solos for the church pianist! You will find the pieces contained in this book to be useful as preludes, offertories, postludes, and concert pieces in some instances.

We've gathered together five fine, talented pianists, composers of note, and contributors to the multifaceted Seasons of Praise project.

Craig Curry, a young, jazz-oriented pianist and worship leader, has provided us with a setting of his lovely and gentle communion chorus "Hungry, I Come." His rhythms, quiet and pervasive, will benefit from a precise performance. The same can be said for the exuberant "Mourning Into Dancing." This is a medium technical challenge, with its tropical feel.

Jim Lucas, new to the family of Fred Bock writers, has provided us with a majestic setting of "Thou Art Worthy," beginning with a fanfare, and flowing into a steady hymn of praise. Jim has also created a simple setting of "Open the Eyes of My Heart, Lord," rhythmic and melodic.

Energy, drive and articulation characterize our ever-popular arrangements by **Mark Hayes**. You will find his settings of "I Want to Be Where You Are," and his own praise song, "No One Like You, O Lord," to be varied and useful.

Joe Martin, a terrific performer and composer, has contributed "Whisper to My Heart" to this collection. As with all his other compositions, this piece is accessible and useful. He has teamed up with his trusted musical partner, *David Angerman* for this arrangement.

"Shout to the Lord" was something I truly enjoyed arranging. You will learn it quickly if you keep the eighth note steady and energizing throughout the meter changes. "Search Me, O God," originally written by Fred Bock as an anthem, is lyrical and introspective. The first section is freestyle, with some interesting harmonics, and then it transitions into a steady ballad feel.

And speaking of **Fred Bock**, we've also included "Give Thanks" which he arranged in 1991. I know you will want to have it in your repertoire.

Jan Sanborn
Keyboard Editor, Fred Bock Music Company

SHOUT TO THE LORD

DARLENE ZSCHECH
Arranged by JAN SANBORN

17
21
poco rall.
25
a tempo
29
33
cresc. poco a poco

37
poco rall.
41
mf a tempo
45
49
53

57
61
64
67
70
molto cresc.

73
f
77
81
1.
86
2.
90
mp cresc. poco a poco
molto rit.

94
Broadly
ff
98
102
1.
107
2.
gradually slowing
and dim. to end
111
115

I WANT TO BE WHERE YOU ARE

DON MOEN
Arranged by MARK HAYES

Gently rhythmic (♩ = ca. 63)

10
12
14
16
18

20
mf
22
24
3
cresc.
f
26
28
mp
mf

30
mf
32
34
36
f
38

40
p
mp
42
44
46
cresc.
48
mf
rit. e dim.
8va
p

MOURNING INTO DANCING

TOMMY WALKER
Arranged by CRAIG CURRY

13
3
16
19
22
mf
25
mp
28

31
mf
34
37
40
f
43
46

49
52
55
58
mf
mp
61

64
mf
67
70
73
ff
76

79
82
85
88
mp
91
f

GIVE THANKS

HENRY SMITH
Arranged by FRED BOCK

17
21
f
25
ff
29
32
l.h.

35
39
ff
42
mf
mp
46
mf
a little faster
ff
50

53
56
60
64
ten.
gradually slowing
ff
f
mf
mp
68
mp
slight accel.
rit.
pp

OPEN THE EYES OF MY HEART

PAUL BALOCHE
Arranged by JIM LUCAS

Moderato, in a light rock ballad style (♩ = 100)

17
3
21
3
25
29
slightly detached
33
8va
8va

37
41
8va
slightly detached
8va
45
Gently
mp
3
49
3
53
mf
3

57
3
61
65
3
69
73
3

Like the beginning, but stronger
rall.
molto rit.

WHISPER TO MY HEART

Music and arrangement by
DAVID ANGERMAN
and JOSEPH M. MARTIN

17
mf
20
23
26
mp
29
allargando
mf
a tempo
rall.

33
mf a tempo
36
38
mp
41
mp
45
dim. e rit.
l.h.

SEARCH ME, O GOD

FRED BOCK
Arranged by JAN SANBORN

26
3
31
36
accel. e cresc. poco a poco
41
rall.
a tempo
mf
46
3

50
54
Freely
mp
poco rall.
58
62
65
rit.

HUNGRY, I COME

Music and Arrangement by
CRAIG CURRY

16
mf
19
22
26
29

32
rit.
mp a tempo
36
f
39
mf
43
rit.
mp a tempo
47
rit.
p

NO ONE LIKE YOU, O LORD

Music and arrangement by
MARK HAYES

16
mf
f
20
24
Ped.
8vb
mp legato
28
32
3
mf

36
3
40
f detached
43
mp legato
46
f detached
3
legato
49
mp
p

53
ff
56
1 2 3 1 2
f
59
62
65

68
71
74
ff
77
f
ff
f
80

83
86
mf
89
92
f
95
ff

THOU ART WORTHY

PAULINE MICHAEL MILLS
Arranged by JIM LUCAS

Majestic, bold and accented (♩ = 76)

37
p
p
mf
mf
41
mf
45
49
rit.
Broader
f
53

57
mf
61
65
p
mp
mf
69
f
73
p
mf
p
mf

77
mf
81
Like the beginning (bold, accented)
f
85
rall.
89
ff
molto rit.
fff